FAT QUARTER
Shuffle™

Edited by Carolyn S. Vagts

Annie's®

Introduction

It seems that fat quarters are like weeds. They spring up in every corner of your sewing room—on shelves, in closets and in half-assembled project storage boxes.

If a quilter loves a certain fabric, but doesn't have a plan in mind for it, buying a fat quarter seems to be the answer. Buy a fat quarter, take it home and look at it. It's sort of like eye candy. But then, before you know what has happened, you have an entire shelf of beautiful fabrics and no plan. Now, if you liked it once, and I'm sure you did, then it's time to revisit your fat-quarter stash. These fat quarters have real possibilities.

Fat Quarter Shuffle is completely dedicated to using those extra fat quarters. Our designers have outdone themselves. You will find 13 projects, all using just six fat quarters (some with the help of a background fabric). Collect and sort your fat quarters, and you'll be amazed at how many you can use with this book. Build your own unique collection from the fabrics you have. This is a book you can use time and time again, and each time you do, the project will be totally different.

Here is the source of inspiration you've been looking for. So gather a six-pack of fat quarters, and let's get started. Do the *Fat Quarter Shuffle*!

Table of Contents

Sassy Classy Tote,
page 12

Six, Slashed Quilt,
page 39

Wingnuts

Designed & Quilted by Tricia Lynn Maloney

Combine four Bow Tie blocks into a larger block unit, set on point with a white background fabric, and you will have a great table topper or possibly a wall hanging.

Specifications
Skill Level: Intermediate
Topper Size: 29½" x 29½"
Block Size: 4½" x 4½" finished
Number of Blocks: 20

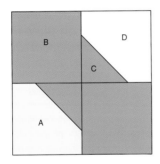

Bow Tie
4½" x 4½" Finished Block
Make 20

Materials
• 6 coordinating fat quarters
• ⅜ yard coordinating binding fabric
• ⅔ yard white solid
• Backing to size
• Batting to size
• Thread
• Basic sewing tools and supplies

Cutting

From 1 fat quarter:
• Select 1 fat quarter as the focal fabric for the A squares used as the four-block centers.
  Cut 3 (2¾" x 21") strips.
    Subcut into 20 (2¾") A squares.
• Cut 1 (2½" x 21") strip.
    Subcut into 4 (2½") G squares.

From each of the remaining 5 fat quarters:
• Cut 2 (2¾" x 21") strips.
    Subcut strips into 8 (2¾") B squares each fabric to total 40 B squares.
• Cut 1 (2" x 21") strip.
    Subcut into 8 (2") C squares each fabric to total 40 C squares.
• Cut 4 (2½" x 4¾") H rectangles from 2 fat quarters to total 8 H rectangles.
• Cut 4 (2½" x 9½") I rectangles from 2 fat quarters to total 8 I rectangles.

From coordinating binding fabric:
• Cut 4 (2¼" by fabric width) strips.

From white solid:
• Cut 2 (2¾" by fabric width) strips.
    Subcut into 20 (2¾") D squares.
• Cut 1 (14" by fabric width) strip.
    Subcut strip into 1 (14") square. Cut the square on both diagonals to make four E triangles. Trim the remainder of the strip to 7¼" and cut 2 (7¼") squares. Cut each square in half on 1 diagonal to make 4 F triangles.

Completing the Blocks
1. Draw a diagonal line from corner to corner on the wrong side of each C square.

2. Referring to Figure 1, place a C square right sides together on one corner of an A square; stitch on the marked line. Trim seam to ¼" and press C to the right side to complete an A-C unit.

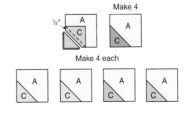

Make 4

Make 4 each

Figure 1

3. Repeat step 2 to complete a total of four A-C units of each color, again referring to Figure 1.

4. Repeat step 2 with C and D pieces to make a total of 20 D-C units (four of each color combination) as shown in Figure 2.

Make 4 each

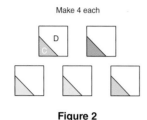

Figure 2

Here's a Tip

Notice that in the sample project, the blue bow tie shapes stand out from the others. Placement of those blocks is important in this project because they are positioned to make them appear to be swirling around the center unit, which does not have any blue in it. Play with the arrangement of the blocks before joining them into four-block units.

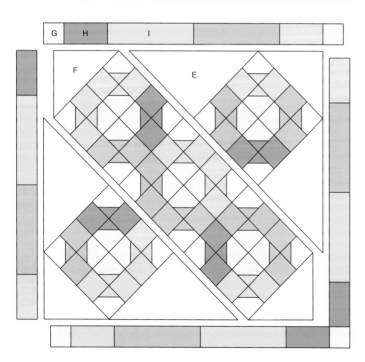

Wingnuts
Assembly Diagram 29½" x 29½"

5. To complete one Bow Tie block, select two matching B squares, and one each A-C and D-C units with C triangles to match the B squares. Arrange and join to complete one Bow Tie block referring to Figure 3; press.

Figure 3

6. Repeat step 5 to complete a total of 20 Bow Tie blocks.

Completing the Topper

1. Select four different Bow Tie blocks. Arrange blocks in a four-block unit as shown in Figure 4. Repeat with remaining Bow Tie blocks to make five four-block units. When satisfied with the arrangements, join the blocks to complete the units; press. *Note: See Tip for block arrangement suggestions.*

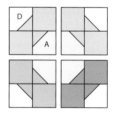

Figure 4

2. Referring to the Assembly Diagram, join the four-block units with the E and F triangles in diagonal rows and then join the rows to complete the pieced center; press seams toward E and F triangles.

3. Join two I strips and add H to each end to make a side strip referring to the Assembly Diagram; press. Repeat to make a total of four side strips.

4. Sew two of these strips to opposite sides of the pieced center; press.

5. Add a G square to each end of each remaining side strip and sew to the remaining sides of the pieced center to complete the pieced top; press.

6. Create a quilt sandwich referring to Finishing Your Quilt on page 48.

7. Quilt as desired.

8. Bind referring to Finishing Your Quilt on page 48 to finish. ∎

"Don't be afraid to use big bold prints in a small quilt." —Tricia Lynn Maloney

The Shuffle

Designed & Quilted by Jenny Rekeweg

It's amazing what you can make with six fat quarters.
This quick and easy project can be made in a day.

Specifications
Skill Level: Confident Beginner
Runner Size: 52" x 24½"

Materials
- 1 fat quarter print
- 5 fat quarters solids to coordinate with the print
- ⅜ yard coordinating solid for binding
- Backing to size
- Batting to size
- Thread
- Basic sewing tools and supplies

Project Note
You will cut a few more pieces than needed to make the runner, but this allows you to move pieces around until you are pleased with the arrangement.

Cutting

From print and solid fat quarters:
- Referring to Figure 1 for best use of each fat quarter, cut the following rectangles from each fat quarter: 6 (3¾" x 6¼") A, 1 (1½" x 3¾") B, 3 (3¾" x 10¼") C, 3 (3½" x 3¾") D and 5 (2" x 3¾") E.

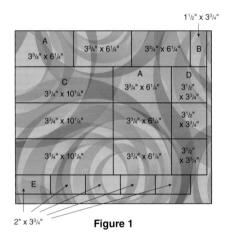

Figure 1

From coordinating solid:
- Cut 4 (2¼" by fabric width) binding strips.

Here's a Tip
It helps to have a design wall to allow you to move pieces around. Take a digital photo of several arrangements and audition the photos before choosing the final layout for pieces.

Completing the Runner
1. Arrange and join 16 of the 18 C rectangles to make a C row referring to the Assembly Diagram, joining rectangles in pairs, then joining the pairs and so on until you have completed the C strip; press seams open. Set aside leftover C rectangles for another project.

2. Repeat step 1 with 16 A rectangles to make an A strip; repeat to make a second A strip.

3. Repeat step 1 with an assortment of the B, D and E rectangles, making sure the stitched strip measures 52½" to fit with the A and C strips.

4. Arrange and join the A, C and B-D-E strips referring to the Assembly Diagram to complete the runner top; press seams open.

5. Create a quilt sandwich referring to Finishing Your Quilt on page 48.

6. Quilt as desired.

7. Bind referring to Finishing Your Quilt on page 48 to finish. ■

"I love using solids, but adding one print that brings the colors all together or adding a focus is always fun. Maybe pick your favorite fat quarter and from that print, find five solids that work with it. The Kaffe Fassett print was my inspiration to find solids to use in this runner." —Jenny Rekeweg

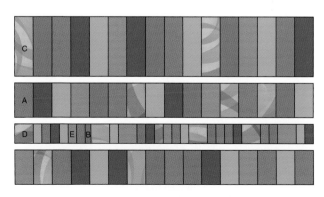

The Shuffle
Assembly Diagram 52" x 24½"

Train Tracks

Designed by Gina Gempesaw
Quilted by Carole Whaling

Select six fat quarters and a background fabric, and you're almost finished. This adorable quilt only has nine blocks, a pieced sashing and a simple border.

Specifications
Skill Level: Intermediate
Quilt Size: 48½" x 48½"
Block Size: 13½" x 13½" finished
Number of Blocks: 9

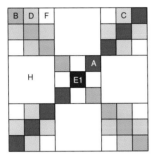

Train Tracks
13½" x 13½" Finished Block
Make 9

Materials
- 1 fat quarter each light and dark pink, light and dark orange, and purple tonals
- 1 fat quarter chevron print
- ½ yard purple solid
- 2 yards white tonal
- Backing to size
- Batting to size
- Thread
- Basic sewing tools and supplies

Cutting

From tonal fat quarters:
- Cut 8 (2" x 21") strips each light (C) and dark (A) pink and light (D) and dark (B) orange tonals.
- Cut 2 (2" x 21") E1 strips purple tonal.
  Subcut 1 strip into 4 (2") E2 squares.

From chevron print:
- Fussy-cut 12 (2" x 8") I strips.

From purple solid:
- Cut 5 (2¼" by fabric width) binding strips.

From white tonal:
- Cut 6 (2" by fabric width) strips.
  Subcut into 12 (2" x 21") F strips.
- Cut 2 (3½" by fabric width) strips.
  Subcut into 24 (2" x 3½") G rectangles.
- Cut 5 (5" by fabric width) strips.
  Subcut into 36 (5") H squares.
- Cut 5 (3" by fabric width) J/K strips.

Completing the Train Tracks Blocks
1. Join one each A, C and F strip along the length to make an A-C-F strip set; press. Repeat to make a total of four A-C-F strip sets.

2. Subcut the A-C-F strip sets into 36 (2" x 5") A-C-F segments referring to Figure 1.

Cut 36
2"

Figure 1

3. Sew a C strip to opposite sides of an A strip along the length to make an A-C strip set; press. Repeat to make a second strip set.

4. Subcut the A-C strip sets into 18 (2" x 5") A-C segments referring to Figure 2.

Cut 18
2"

Figure 2

5. Join one each B, D and F strip to make a B-D-F strip set; press; Repeat to make a total of four strip sets.

6. Subcut the B-D-F strip sets into 36 (2" x 5") B-D-F segments referring to Figure 3.

Figure 3

7. Sew a B strip between two D strips along the length to make a B-D strip set; press. Repeat to make a second strip set.

8. Subcut the B-D strip sets into 18 (2" x 5") B-D units as shown in Figure 4.

Figure 4

9. Join one each A, F and B strip along the length to make an A-F-B strip set; press. Repeat to make a second strip set.

10. Subcut the A-F-B strip sets into 18 (2" x 5") A-F-B segments referring to Figure 5.

Figure 5

11. Sew an F strip to opposite sides of E1 along the length to make an E-F strip set; press. Subcut the strip set into nine 2" x 5" E-F segments as shown in Figure 6.

Figure 6

12. Select and join one A-C segment and two A-C-F segments to complete a pink unit as shown in Figure 7; press. Repeat to make a total of 18 pink units.

Figure 7

13. Select and join one B-D segment with two B-D-F segments to make a orange unit as shown in Figure 8; press. Repeat to make a total of 18 orange units.

Figure 8

14. Sew an E-F segment between two A-F-B segments to make a center unit as shown in Figure 9; press. Repeat to make a total of nine center units.

Figure 9

15. Select, arrange and join two each pink and orange units with one center unit and four H squares to make rows referring to Figure 10; press seams toward H.

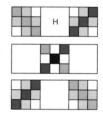

Figure 10

16. Join the rows to complete one Train Tracks block; press.

17. Repeat steps 15 and 16 to complete a total of nine Train Tracks blocks.

Completing the Quilt

1. Sew a G rectangle to each end of each I strip to make 12 G-I units as shown in Figure 11; press seams toward I.

Figure 11

2. Arrange and join three Train Tracks blocks with two G-I units to make a block row referring to the Assembly Diagram; press seams toward the G-I units. Repeat to make three block rows.

3. Arrange and join three G-I units and two E2 squares to make a sashing row referring to the Assembly Diagram; press. Repeat to make a second sashing row.

4. Join the block rows and the sashing rows referring to the Assembly Diagram to complete the pieced center; press seams toward sashing rows.

5. Join the J/K strips on the short ends to make one long strip; press. Subcut strip into two 3" x 44" J strips and two 3" x 49" K strips.

6. Sew J strips to the top and bottom, and K strips to opposite sides of the pieced center to complete the quilt top; press seams toward strips.

7. Create a quilt sandwich referring to Finishing Your Quilt on page 48.

8. Quilt as desired.

9. Bind referring to Finishing Your Quilt on page 48 to finish. ■

Here's a Tip

To keep the chevron pattern in the chevron print perfectly straight, the sashing strips will need to be fussy-cut one at a time. Select an area of the print and align the lines of your rotary ruler at the tips of a chevron to keep the design straight when cutting.

"I found this chevron print very intriguing, so this quilt is inspired by the colors and pattern in this print."
—Gina Gempesaw

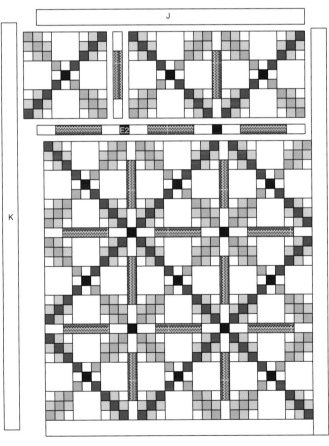

Train Tracks Alternate Size
Assembly Diagram 48½" x 63½"
Add another row of 3 blocks & another sashing row to make a lap-size quilt. Remember to purchase more fabrics for this option.

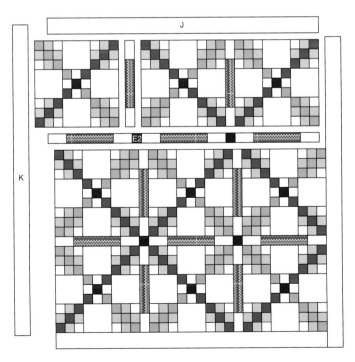

Train Tracks
Assembly Diagram 48½" x 48½"

Sassy Classy Tote

Designed & Quilted by Tricia Lynn Maloney

Fat quarters are the perfect choice for this stylish tote with hidden pockets. Dig out your fat quarters and make several for yourself or for your friends.

Specifications

Skill Level: Confident Beginner
Tote Size: 12" x 14" x 4", excluding handles

Materials

- 6 coordinating fat quarters
- ½ yard coordinating lining fabric
- ¾ yard fusible fleece
- Thread
- Large hair elastic
- Large coordinating button
- Basic sewing tools and supplies

Cutting

Assign a number to each fat quarter (1–6).

From fat quarter 1:

- Cut 2 (6½" x 14½") A front and back panel rectangles.
- Cut 1 (5½" x 12½" E1) inside pocket rectangle.

From fat quarter 2:

- Cut 2 (6½" x 7½") B outer pocket rectangles.

From fat quarter 3:

- Cut 4 (6½" x 7½") C outer pocket lining rectangles.

From fat quarter 4:

- Cut 2 (6½" x 7½") D rectangles for crazy-pieced panel foundations.
- Cut 1 (5½" x 12½") E2 rectangle for inside pocket lining.

From fat quarter 5:

- Cut 1 (4½" x 12½") F1 bottom gusset rectangle.
- Cut 2 (4½" x 14½") G1 side gusset rectangles.

From fat quarter 6:

- Cut 2 (4½" x 21") H strips for handles.

From coordinating lining fabric:

- Cut 2 (12½" x 14½") front and back rectangles.
- Cut 1 (4½" x 12½") F2 bottom gusset.
- Cut 2 (4½" x 14½") G2 side gussets.

From fusible fleece:

- Cut 2 (12½" x 14½") front and back rectangles.
- Cut 2 (6½" x 7½") B outer pocket rectangles.
- Cut 1 (5½" x 12½") E inner pocket rectangle.
- Cut 2 (4½" x 21") H handle strips.
- Cut 1 (4½" x 12½") F bottom gusset.
- Cut 2 (4½" x 14½") G side gussets.

Completing the Crazy Patchwork

1. Cut assorted shapes from the remainder of fat quarters for crazy piecing.

2. Select one D rectangle and two fabric shapes cut for crazy piecing.

3. Referring to Figure 1, place the two fabric shapes right sides together on the wrong side of D and stitch; press the top piece to the right side.

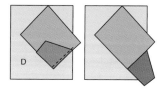

Figure 1

4. Repeat step 3 with more cut shapes until the D square is completely covered, referring to Figure 2.

 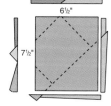

Figure 2   **Figure 3**

5. Turn the pieced D panel with the crazy-pieced side down and trim excess fabric even with D referring to Figure 3. The D panel should measure 6½" x 7½".

6. Repeat steps 2–5 to complete a second D panel.

Completing the Tote Front & Back

1. Fuse a fusible fleece B rectangle to the wrong side of one fabric B outer pocket rectangle.

2. Layer the fused B rectangle right sides together with a C pocket lining rectangle right sides together. Stitch across one 6½" edge.

3. Turn right side out; press top edge flat and topstitch close to the stitched top edge to complete one B outer pocket as shown in Figure 4.

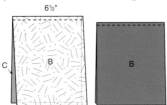

Figure 4

4. Repeat steps 1–3 to complete a second B outer pocket.

5. Sew a D panel to a C lining rectangle along the 6½" bottom edge of D to make a front side panel as shown in Figure 5; press. Repeat to make the back side panel.

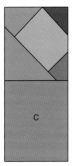 

Figure 5   Figure 6

6. Layer and pin one B outer pocket completed in steps 1–3 right side up on the C-D front side panel; baste across bottom edge of pocket as shown in Figure 6.

7. Sew an A rectangle to the left-side edge of the B-C-D front side panel to complete the tote front as shown in Figure 7; press seam toward A.

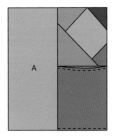

Figure 7

8. Repeat steps 6 and 7 to complete the tote back.

9. Fuse a 12½" x 14½" rectangle fusible fleece to the wrong side of the tote front and back pieces.

Completing the Tote

1. Fuse the fusible fleece pieces to the wrong side of the matching size E1, F1 and G1 pieces.

2. Sew the F gusset between two G gussets to make the gusset strip, stopping stitching at the end of the ¼" seam allowance at both ends of each strip as shown in Figure 8; press seams open.

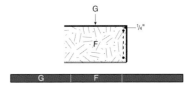

Figure 8

3. Sew the F-G gusset strip to the side and bottom edges of the assembled front, stopping stitching at the ¼" seam allowance to turn corners as shown in Figure 9. Secure stitching at beginning and end of seams; press.

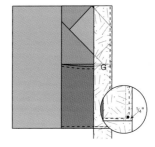

Figure 9

4. Repeat step 3 with the side and bottom edges of the assembled back to complete the outer bag.

5. Fuse a fusible fleece H strip to the wrong side of each H handle strip.

6. Referring to Figure 10, fold one H strip in half along length with wrong sides together and press. Unfold and fold both long edges to the creased center fold. Refold the strip on the original center fold and pin edges together to hold. Sew ⅛" away from the long edges on both long sides of the strip to complete one handle.

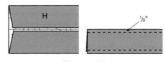

Figure 10

7. Repeat step 6 to complete the second handle.

8. Pin and machine-baste a handle to the right side of the tote front, position each end 3" from the center seam as shown in Figure 11; repeat on top of tote back with second handle.

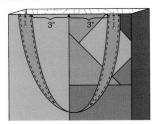

Figure 11

9. Center the large hair elastic at the top right side of the tote back between the handles and machine-baste to hold in place as shown in Figure 12.

Figure 12

10. Layer a fused E1 inside pocket with the E2 inside pocket lining piece, right sides together and sew along both 12½" edges; turn right side out and press. Topstitch close to the top long edge of the pocket.

11. Place the inside pocket on the back lining piece about 4½" above the bottom edge, aligning left and right raw edges. Pin and then sew ⅛" from the bottom of the pocket edge referring to Figure 13.

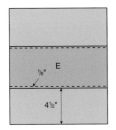

Figure 13

12. Mark and stitch desired pocket divisions, securing stitches at the beginning and end.

13. Repeat steps 2–4 with lining front and back rectangles and lining bottom and side gusset (F2 and G2) strips to complete the tote lining, leaving a 6" opening in one bottom seam for turning.

14. Insert the stitched outer tote into the lining tote with right sides together, matching seams at the top edge; stitch all around top edge.

15. Turn the tote right side out through the opening left in the lining and push lining inside tote; press top edge flat and topstitch close to the edge.

16. Hand- or machine-stitch lining opening closed.

17. Hand-stitch the button on the front top edge, aligning with the stitched hair elastic for closing to finish. ∎

"This tote was inspired by the crazy-pieced panel accent. A funky button can make all the difference." —Tricia Lynn Maloney

Here's a Tip

If you are using light-color fat quarters, be sure to select a light color for the foundation square. A dark fabric or one with a print might show through the crazy-pieced patchwork. You may want to select muslin or use just a batting square for the foundation.

Sassy Classy Tote
Placement Diagram 12" x 14" x 4", excluding handles

Stunning Stars

Designed by Nancy Scott
Quilted by Masterpiece Quilting

This variation of a Friendship Star block, a six-pack of
fat quarters and a background fabric make the perfect
lap quilt or, with the right fabrics, a fun baby quilt.

Specifications

Skill Level: Confident Beginner
Quilt Size: 39" x 48"
Block Size: 9" x 9" finished
Number of Blocks: 12

Materials

- 1 fat quarter dark purple tonal
- 1 fat quarter aqua print
- 4 fat quarters pastel tonal
- 2 yards white solid
- Backing to size
- Batting to size
- Thread
- Basic sewing tools and supplies

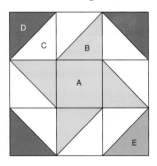

Corner Star
9" x 9" Finished Block
Make 4

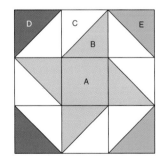

Side Star
9" x 9" Finished Block
Make 6

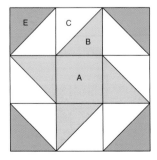

Friendship Star
9" x 9" Finished Block
Make 2

Cutting

From dark purple tonal:
- Cut 3 (3⅞" x 21") strips.
  Subcut into 12 (3⅞") D squares.

From aqua print:
- Cut 3 (3⅞" x 21") strips.
  Subcut into 12 (3⅞") E squares.

From 1 pastel tonal:
- Cut 9 (1½" x 21") H/I strips.

From 3 remaining pastel tonals:
- Cut 1 (3½" x 21") strip.
  Subcut into 4 (3½") A squares each fabric
    to total 12.
- Cut 2 (3⅞" x 21") strips.
  Subcut into 8 (3⅞") B squares each fabric
    to total 24.

From white solid:
- Cut 1 piece 45" by fabric width.
  Subcut along length into 4 (2½" x 45") strips.
    Trim strips to make 2 (2½" x 36½") F strips and
    2 (2½" x 31½") G strips.
  From the remaining 45" piece, cut 4 (3½" x 45")
    J/K strips along length. Trim strips to make 2
    (3½" x 42½") J strips and 2 (3½" x 39½") K strips.
  From the remaining 45" piece, cut 5 (2¼" x 45")
    binding strips along length.
  Subcut the remainder of the 45" piece into
    11 (3⅞") C squares.
- Cut 4 (3⅞" by fabric width) strips from the
  remaining yardage.
    Subcut into an additional 37 (3⅞") C squares
    (total 48 C squares).

Completing the Blocks

1. Draw a diagonal line from corner to corner on the
wrong side of each C square.

Fat Quarter Shuffle

2. Referring to Figure 1, place a C square right sides together with a B square and stitch ¼" on each side of the marked line; cut apart on the marked line and press the units open with seams away from C to complete two B-C units. Repeat with all B squares to complete a total of 48 B-C units.

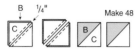

Figure 1

3. Repeat step 2 with C and D to make 24 C-D units and with C and E to make 24 C-E units referring to Figure 2.

Figure 2

4. Select one A square, four B-C units to match A and four C–E units to make a Friendship Star block.

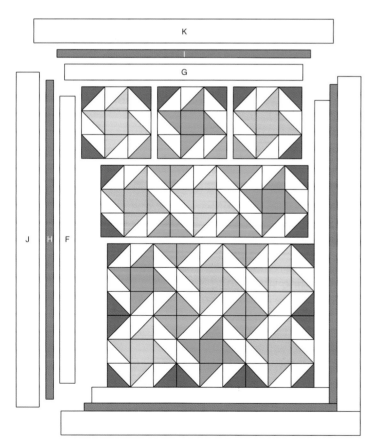

Stunning Stars
Assembly Diagram 39" x 48"

5. Sew a B-C unit to opposite sides of A to make the center row referring to Figure 3; press seams toward A.

Figure 3

6. Sew a C-E unit to opposite sides of a B-C unit to make the top row as shown in Figure 4; press seams toward C-E. Repeat to make the bottom row.

Figure 4

7. Join the rows referring to Figure 5 to complete one block; press.

Figure 5

8. Repeat steps 4–7 to complete a second block.

9. Select one A square, four B-C units to match A, one C-E unit and three C-D units to complete one Corner Star block.

10. Refer to steps 5–7 and Figure 6 to complete one block; press. Repeat to make a total of four Corner Star blocks.

Figure 6

11. Select one A square, four B-C units to match A and two each C-E units and C-D units to complete one Side Star block.

12. Refer to steps 5–7 and Figure 7 to complete one block; press. Repeat to make a total of six Side Star blocks.

Figure 7

Completing the Quilt

1. Arrange and join the Friendship Star, Corner Star and Side Star blocks in four rows of three blocks each referring to the Assembly Diagram; press.

2. Join the rows to complete the pieced center; press.

3. Sew F strips to opposite long sides and G strips to the top and bottom of the pieced center; press seams toward strips.

4. Join the H/I strips on the short ends with diagonal seams as shown in Figure 8; press seams open. Subcut strip into two 1½" x 40½" H strips and two 1½" x 33½" I strips.

Figure 8

5. Sew H strips to opposite long sides and I strips to the top and bottom of the pieced center; press seam toward strips.

6. Sew J strips to opposite long sides and K strips to the top and bottom of the pieced center to complete the quilt top; press seams toward strips.

7. Create a quilt sandwich referring to Finishing Your Quilt on page 48.

8. Quilt as desired.

9. Bind referring to Finishing Your Quilt on page 48 to finish. ■

"The Friendship Star has always been one of my favorite block patterns. The addition of the extra half-square triangles creates a secondary pattern that makes the stars even more stunning." —Nancy Scott

Here's a Tip

Cut border strips along the length of the fabric to avoid any stretching that causes wavy borders. After cutting these strips, the remainder of the fabric width may be used to cut other pieces needed from the same fabric. In this case, the longest border strips are cut 42½". More than just the remainder of the fabric is needed, so the border strip lengths are cut first, the remainder of the fabric width is cut into other pieces and then the remaining yardage is cut into fabric-width strips as needed.

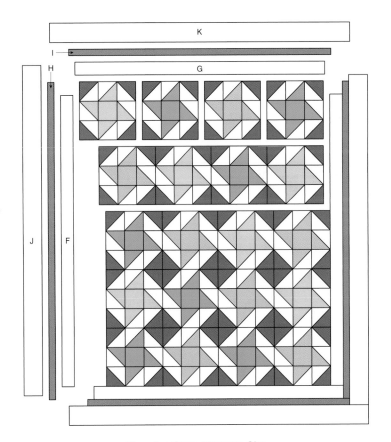

Stunning Stars Alternate Size
Assembly Diagram 48" x 57"
Add another row to the side & another row at the bottom to make a lap-size quilt. Remember to purchase more fabric for this option.

Raining Boxes

Designed by Bev Getschel
Quilted by Lynette Gelling

These traditional blocks take on a whole new look when set on point in an asymmetrical setting with a white background fabric.

Specifications
Skill Level: Confident Beginner
Quilt Size: 54⅞" x 70½"
Block Size: 9" x 9" finished
Number of Blocks: 15

Materials
- 1 fat quarter each medium gray, yellow, red, purple, turquoise and lime green solids
- ⅝ yard medium gray solid
- 4¼ yards white solid
- Backing to size
- Batting to size
- Thread
- Basic sewing tools and supplies

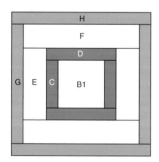

Framed Box 1
9" x 9" Finished Block
Make 5

Box on Point
9" x 9" Finished Block
Make 8

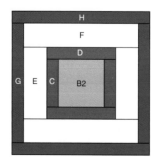

Framed Box 2
9" x 9" Finished Block
Make 2

Cutting
From fat quarters:
- Cut 1 (3½") B2 square each from 2 fat quarters.
- Cut 2 (2½" x 21") strips from each fat quarter to total 12 strips.
   Subcut into a total of 73 (2½") A squares and 8 (2⅜") X squares.
- Select 2 colors for the box colors for each Framed Box 1 and 2 block.
   Cut 2 each 1¼" x 3½" C and 1¼" x 5" D strips from 1 color.
   Cut 2 each 1¼" x 8" G and 1¼" x 9½" H strips from the second color.
   Repeat with different colors to cut C and D strips and G and H strips for a total of 7 blocks.
- Select 1 color for each Box on Point block.
   Cut 2 each 1¼" x 5⅜" K and 1¼" x 6⅞" L strips.
   Repeat to cut K and L strips from different colors for a total of 8 blocks.

From medium gray solid:
- Cut 7 (2¼" by fabric width) binding strips.

From white solid:
- Cut 1 (14" by fabric width) strip.
   Subcut into 3 (14") squares. Cut each square on both diagonals to make a total of 12 R side triangles; set aside 2 for another project.
- Cut 1 (13" by fabric width) strip.
   Subcut into 6 (2½" x 13") P strips, 2 (10⅛") Q squares and 4 (2½") O squares. Cut each Q square in half on 1 diagonal to make 4 corner Q triangles.
- Cut 3 (9½" by fabric width) strips.
   Subcut into 38 (2½" x 9½") N strips and 2 (4½" x 25⅜") T strips.
- Cut 2 (4½" by fabric width) strips.
   Subcut into 2 (4½" x 35") V strips.
- Cut 1 (3½" by fabric width) strip.
   Subcut into 5 (3½") B1 squares.

- Cut 4 (2½" by fabric width) strips.
  Subcut into 2 each 2½" x 22½" S strips and
  2½" x 34½" U strips.
- Cut 1 (5" by fabric width) strip.
  Subcut into 14 (2" x 5") E rectangles.
- Cut 1 (8" by fabric width) strip.
  Subcut into 14 (2" x 8") F rectangles.
- Cut 1 (9½" by fabric width) strip.
  Subcut into 3 (9½") W squares.
- Cut 4 (7¼" by fabric width) strips.
  Subcut into 16 (7¼") squares. Cut each square
    in half on 1 diagonal to make 32 M triangles.
- Cut 1 (2⅜" by fabric width) strip.
  Subcut into 16 (2" x 2⅜") I rectangles.
- Cut 1 (5⅜" by fabric width) strip.
  Subcut into 16 (2" x 5⅜") J rectangles.

Completing the Framed Box Blocks

1. Select two matching C and D strips and two matching G and H strips, one B1 square and two each E and F strips to complete one Framed Box 1 block.

2. Sew C to opposite sides and D to the remaining sides of B1 referring to Figure 1; press.

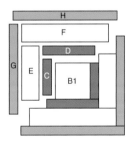

Figure 1

3. Sew E to opposite sides and F to remaining sides of the stitched unit; press.

4. Sew G to opposite sides and H to the remaining sides of the pieced unit to complete one Framed Box 1 block, again referring to Figure 1; press.

5. Repeat steps 1–4 to complete a total of five Framed Box 1 blocks and two Framed Box 2 blocks using B2 for the center square referring to the Framed Box 2 block drawing.

Completing the Box on Point Blocks

1. Select one X square and two matching K and L strips, two I rectangles, two J strips and four M triangles for one Box on Point block.

2. Sew I to opposite sides of X and add J to complete the block center referring to Figure 2; press.

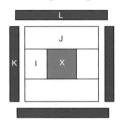

Figure 2

3. Sew K to opposite sides and L to the remaining sides, again referring to Figure 2; press.

4. Sew an M triangle to each side of the pieced unit referring to Figure 3 to complete one Box on Point block; press.

Figure 3

5. Repeat steps 1–4 to complete a total of eight Box on Point blocks.

Completing the Quilt

1. Arrange and join the pieced blocks with the W, A and O squares, the N and P strips, and the Q and R triangles in diagonal rows referring to the Assembly Diagram, with the P strips extending a bit beyond the edges of R as shown in Figure 4; press.

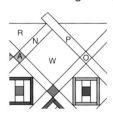

Figure 4

2. Join the rows as pieced; press. Trim excess P strips even with the R triangles referring to Figure 5.

Figure 5

3. Join 11 A squares to make a pieced strip; press. Repeat to make a second pieced strip. Sew each pieced strip to an S strip; press.

4. Sew a pieced S strip to T to make the top strip; press. Repeat to make the bottom strip. Sew these strips to the top and bottom of the pieced center.

5. Join 18 A squares to make a pieced strip; press. Repeat to make a second pieced strip. Sew an A square to one end of a U strip; press. Join the two pieced strips; press. Repeat to make a second pieced strip.

6. Sew a V strip to one end of each pieced strip to make the side strips; press.

7. Sew a side strip to opposite sides of the pieced center to complete the quilt top; press.

8. Create a quilt sandwich referring to Finishing Your Quilt on page 48.

9. Quilt as desired.

10. Bind referring to Finishing Your Quilt on page 48 to finish. ■

"Just because you only have six fat quarters doesn't mean your project has to be small—add more white! Modern quilts and the young, modern quilters inspired me to design this quilt." —Bev Getschel

Raining Boxes
Assembly Diagram 54⁷/₈" x 70½"

A Lapful of Empty Spools

Designed by Connie Kauffman
Quilted by Vickie Hunsberger

When put together with the right color placement, the Snowball Variation blocks create spools.

Specifications
Skill Level: Intermediate
Quilt Size: 49" x 67"
Block Size: 6" x 6" finished
Number of Blocks: 48

Materials
- 1 fat quarter each orange, cream, red, purple, green and blue batiks
- ⅝ yard black/green/orange batik
- 2⅞ yards black batik
- Backing to size
- Batting to size
- Thread
- Basic sewing tools and supplies

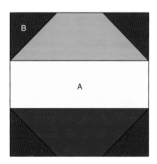

Center Snowball Variation
6" x 6" Finished Block
Make 28

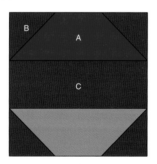

Border Snowball Variation
6" x 6" Finished Block
Make 8

Border Stripe
6" x 6" Finished Block
Make 12

Project Note
In order for the blocks and units to create spool shapes, the color placement within the blocks and the block placement are planned.

Cutting
From fat quarters:
- Cut each fat quarter into 7 (2½" x 21") strips.
  Subcut into 2½" x 6½" A rectangles as follows: 21 each red and purple, 20 each cream and blue, and 19 each green and orange.

From black/green/orange batik:
- Cut 6 (2¼" by fabric width) binding strips.

From black batik:
- Cut 10 (2½" by fabric width) strips.
  Subcut strips into 160 (2½") B squares.
- Cut 1 (6½" by fabric width) strip.
  Subcut into 2 (6½") F squares and 2 (6½" x 12½") G rectangles.
- Cut the following along the remaining length of fabric: 2 each 2½" x 42½" D, 2½" x 28½" E, 5" x 58½" H and 5" x 59½" I; and 4 (2½" x 60") C strips.
  Subcut C strips into 32 (2½" x 6½") C rectangles.

Completing the Center Snowball Variation Blocks
1. Select one each green, purple and blue A rectangle and join to make an A unit as shown in Figure 1; press. Repeat to make a total of three units.

Make 3

Figure 1

2. Repeat step 1 to make two of each A unit in the color combinations shown in Figure 2.

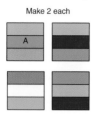

Make 2 each

Figure 2

3. Repeat step 1 to make 1 of each A unit in the color combinations shown in Figure 3.

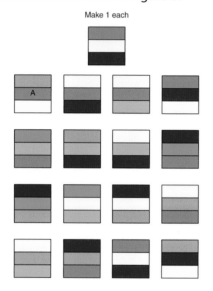

Make 1 each

Figure 3

4. Mark a diagonal line from corner to corner on the wrong side of each B square. Set aside 48 marked B squares for border blocks and units.

5. Place a B square right sides together on each corner of one A unit and stitch on the marked lines as shown in Figure 4.

Figure 4   **Figure 5**

6. Trim seam to ¼" and press B to the right side to complete one Center Snowball Variation block referring to Figure 5.

7. Repeat steps 5 and 6 with the remaining A units to complete a total of 28 Center Snowball Variation blocks.

Completing the Border Stripe Blocks

1. Select one blue A and two C rectangles; sew C to opposite sides of A to complete one blue Border Stripe block referring to Figure 6; press seams toward C.

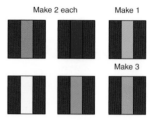

Make 2 each   Make 1

Make 3

Figure 6

2. Repeat step 1 to make two each red, cream, green and purple, and three orange Border Stripe blocks again referring to Figure 6.

Completing the Border Snowball Variation Blocks

1. Sew a C rectangle between one each cream and orange A rectangle to make a cream/orange A-C unit as shown in Figure 7; press. Repeat to make a second cream/orange unit.

Make 2

Figure 7

2. Repeat step 1 to make a total of six more A-C units in the color combinations shown in Figure 8.

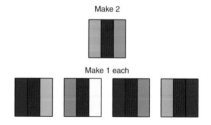

Make 2

Make 1 each

Figure 8

3. Using set-aside B squares, sew a marked B square to each corner of each A-C unit referring to Figures 4 and 5, and steps 5 and 6 of Completing the Center Snowball Variation Blocks to complete the Border Snowball Variation blocks.

Completing the Quilt

1. Referring to the Assembly Diagram, arrange and join the 28 Center Snowball Variation blocks in seven rows of four blocks each; press. ***Note:** Be careful when arranging the block colors to create the spool designs.*

2. Join the rows as pieced to complete the quilt center; press.

3. Sew D strips to opposite sides and E strips to the top and bottom of the quilt center; press seams toward strips.

4. Sew marked B squares to each end of each remaining A rectangle referring to Figures 4 and 5 and steps 5 and 6 of Completing the Center Snowball Variation Blocks to complete eight A-B border units as shown in Figure 9.

Figure 9

5. Arrange and join three each Border Stripe and Border Snowball Variation blocks with two A-B border units to make a side strip referring to the Assembly Diagram for positioning of blocks and units by color; press. Repeat to make a second side strip. Sew these strips to opposite long sides of the quilt center; press seams toward D strips.

6. Arrange and join one Border Snowball Variation and two Border Stripe blocks with two A-B border units and one each F square and G rectangle to make the top strip referring to the Assembly Diagram for positioning of blocks and units by color. Sew this strip to the top of the quilt center; press seam toward E.

7. Repeat step 6 to make the bottom strip. Sew this strip to the bottom of the quilt center; press seam toward E.

8. Sew H strips to opposite long sides and I strips to the top and bottom of the quilt center to complete the quilt top; press seams toward H and I strips.

9. Create a quilt sandwich referring to Finishing Your Quilt on page 48.

10. Quilt as desired.

11. Bind referring to Finishing Your Quilt on page 48 to finish. ∎

"I designed this quilt initially to look like empty spools. As the design evolved, the blocks were simple Snowball blocks and easy to construct." —Connie Kauffman

A Lapful of Empty Spools
Assembly Diagram 49" x 67"

Bountiful Bloom

Designed & Quilted by Jackie White

Try this exciting 3-D technique and create a stunning flower wall hanging for every season.

Specifications
Skill Level: Confident Beginner
Wall Hanging Size: 17" x 20"

Materials
- 2 fat quarters for large petals
- 2 fat quarters for small petals, twirlies and center
- 1 fat quarter for background
- 1 fat quarter for backing
- ⅓ yard coordinating fabric for binding
- Batting to size
- Thread
- 2 sheets 12" x 18" matching color craft foam
- 3½" x 13" rectangle fusible web
- Template materials
- Hot-glue gun
- Small dowel or pencil
- Basic sewing tools and supplies

Cutting
Prepare templates for petals using patterns given. Prepare a second template for each petal using the dashed line marked on the inside of each petal pattern for the craft foam cutting line. Cut as per instructions.

From fat quarters:
- Cut 1 (17½" x 20½") rectangle from 1 fat quarter for background.
- Cut 1 (17½" x 20½") from a second fat quarter for backing.

From coordinating binding fabric:
- Cut 3 (2¼" by fabric width) binding strips.

From craft foam:
- Cut 3 (¼" x 12") strips craft foam.
- Cut for petals as per instructions.

Completing the Petals
1. Lay two fat quarters right sides together and trace the large petal on the top layer 10 times leaving ¼" between pieces and alternating ends of petals to make best use of space.

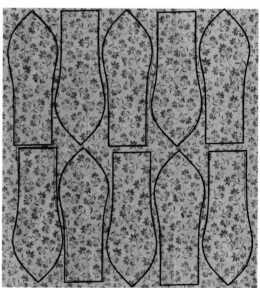

2. Place pins inside each petal shape to hold the layers together.

3. Stitch around each petal on the marked lines, leaving the bottom straight edge open; cut out each petal leaving a narrow seam allowance all around. Clip curves.

4. Turn petals right side out, pushing out points and smoothing curves; press.

5. Trace 10 large petals on the craft foam using the second smaller large petal template; cut out on traced lines.

6. Roll up each long side of a craft foam petal and insert into a fabric petal. Manipulate to lay flat. *Note: If the foam doesn't lie flat, simply pull it out, trim a bit smaller and reinsert.* Repeat for all large petals.

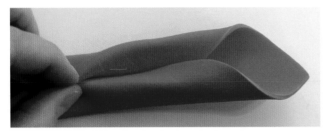

7. Fold the bottom of each petal to the inside to form a triangle or point and pin to hold.

8. Machine-stitch around a petal a generous ¼" from the edge all around, catching the bottom folded point in the stitching. Repeat stitching in consecutive ¼" increments to complete the petal quilting. Repeat for all petals.

9. Press the front of one petal for 10–15 seconds with iron on high setting and no steam, moving the iron constantly to avoid scorching the fabric. Remove the petal and wrap the lower part of the petal around a large marker or piece of dowel

and bend the tip back; hold for 20 seconds. Release and you will have shaped the petal. Repeat for all 10 petals.

10. Repeat steps 1–8 with the small petal templates to make four small petals.

11. To shape the small petals, press as in step 9 and then wrap the large end of the petal around a marker or dowel, curling in to the base of the petal and hold until cool.

Completing the Twirlies

1. Cut a 3½" x 13" strip of leftover fabric; apply fusible web to the wrong side of the strip. Subcut strip into three 1⅛" x 13" strips.

2. Center one ¼" x 12" strip of craft foam on the wrong side of one 1⅛" x 13" strip with each end of the foam ½" from the narrow ends of fabric.

3. Cut each end of the fabric to leave a ½" tab from each end referring to the photo.

4. Heat iron to cotton setting; fold the fabric tab at each end onto the foam strip and press. Moving along the length of the piece, fold one side of the fabric onto the craft foam and then the other side and press.

5. With seam side facing in, wrap the pressed fabric/foam strip around a piece of dowel or pencil. Place iron on it for 10 seconds, rotate for another 10 seconds. Let cool on the dowel/pencil for 15 seconds and release to complete one twirlie.

6. Repeat steps 2–5 to complete a total of three twirlies.

Scrap & Slash Flower Center

1. Cut eight 2" x 12" strips from leftover fat quarters.

2. Fold one strip along length with wrong sides together; stitch a ⅛" seam along the long edge. Repeat with remaining strips.

3. Cut slits about ½" deep and ½" apart along the folded edge of each strip.

4. Select one strip for the center; roll up the strip, dabbing glue at the raw-edge side every inch or so. As you finish rolling one strip, pick up another and continue rolling and adding strips until the flower center is desired size. *Note: The flower center on the sample is approximately 3".*

Completing the Wall Quilt

1. Create a quilt sandwich with the background, backing and batting pieces referring to Finishing Your Quilt on page 48.

2. Quilt as desired.

3. Bind referring to Finishing Your Quilt on page 48 to complete the wall quilt background.

4. Center, arrange and pin the large petals in a pleasing manner, leaving a 2" circle in the center. Hand-stitch in place at each base. Tack the center of each petal in place about 2½" from the base.

5. Repeat step 4 with the rolled small petals.

6. Tack the bases of the twirlies close to the center between petals.

7. Glue the flower center in place to finish.

8. Add a hanging sleeve, rings or hanging loops to the back side for hanging if desired. ■

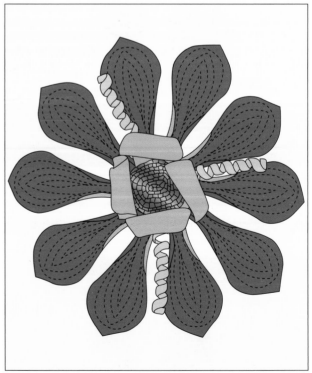

Bountiful Bloom
Placement Diagram 17" x 20"

"I love 3-D embellishing. What better way to create a beautiful flower quilt than to have it have its own 3-D shape?" —Jackie White

Here's a Tip

To make quick hanging loops that won't show, cut three ¾" x 4½" strips along the selvage edge of fabric. Fold each strip in half with wrong sides together to make a loop. Hand-stitch a loop at each end and in the center of the wall quilt with the folded end of each loop 2¾" down from the top edge on the back side of the quilt.

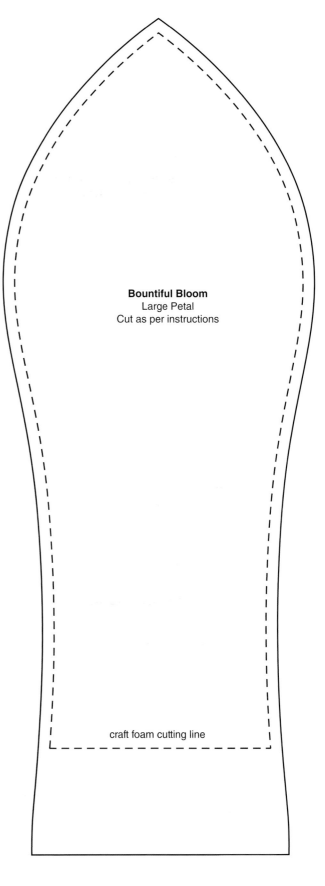

Bountiful Bloom
Large Petal
Cut as per instructions

craft foam cutting line

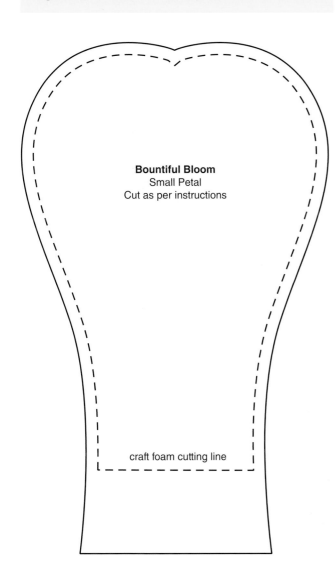

Bountiful Bloom
Small Petal
Cut as per instructions

craft foam cutting line

Starry Dance

Designed & Quilted by Wendy Sheppard

If you've got six fat quarters you absolutely love and want to make a quilt, just add a background fabric and you can. That's all this quilt needs.

Specifications

Skill Level: Intermediate
Quilt Size: 42" x 50"
Block Size: 8" x 8" finished
Number of Blocks: 27

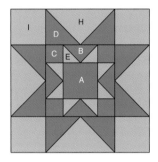

Star-in-a-Star
8" x 8" Finished Block
Make 10

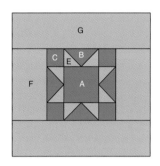

Framed Star
8" x 8" Finished Block
Make 17

Materials

- 1 fat quarter each light blue polka dot, blue solid, green vine print, light green tonal, aqua/orange print, blue floral
- ½ yard coordinating binding fabric
- 2⅓ yards gray solid
- Backing to size
- Batting to size
- Thread
- Basic sewing tools and supplies

Cutting

From light blue polka dot:
- Cut 2 (1½" x 21") strips.
  Subcut into 16 (1½") C squares.
- Cut 1 (2½" x 21") strip.
  Subcut into 4 (2½") A squares.
- Cut 1 (3¼" x 21") strip.
  Subcut into 4 (3¼") B squares.
- Cut 2 (2⅞" x 21") strips.
  Subcut into 12 (2⅞") D squares.

From blue solid:
- Cut 2 (1½" x 21") strips.
  Subcut into 22 (1½") C squares.
- Cut 1 (2½" x 21") strip.
  Subcut into 5 (2½") A squares and 2 (1½" x 2½") J rectangles.
- Cut 1 (3¼" x 21") strip.
  Subcut into 5 (3¼") B squares and 1 (1⅞") K square.
- Cut 2 (2⅞" x 21") strips.
  Subcut into 8 (2⅞") D squares.

From green vine print:
- Cut 2 (1½" x 21") strips.
  Subcut into 22 (1½") C squares.
- Cut 1 (2½" x 21") strip.
  Subcut into 7 (2½") A squares and 2 (1½" x 2½") J rectangles.
- Cut 1 (3¼" x 21") strip.
  Subcut into 5 (3¼") B squares and 1 (1⅞") K square.
- Cut 1 (2⅞" x 21") strip.
  Subcut into 5 (2⅞") D squares.

From light green tonal:
- Cut 2 (1½" x 21") strips.
  Subcut into 20 (1½") C squares.
- Cut 1 (2½" x 21") strip.
  Subcut into 6 (2½") A squares and 4 (1½" x 2½") J rectangles.
- Cut 1 (3¼" x 21") strip.
  Subcut into 4 (3¼") B squares and 2 (1⅞") K squares.
- Cut 1 (2⅞" x 21") strip.
  Subcut into 5 (2⅞") D squares.

From aqua/orange print:
- Cut 1 (1½" x 21") strip.
  Subcut into 14 (1½") C squares.
- Cut 1 (2½" x 21") strip.
  Subcut into 3 (2½") A squares, 2 (1½" x 2½") J rectangles and 1 (1⅞") K square.

- Cut 1 (3¼" x 21") strip.
  Subcut into 3 (3¼") B squares.
- Cut 2 (2⅞" x 21") strips.
  Subcut into 8 (2⅞") D squares.

From blue floral:
- Cut 2 (1½" x 21") strips.
  Subcut into 26 (1½") C squares.
- Cut 2 (2½" x 21") strips.
  Subcut into 8 (2½") A squares and
    2 (1½" x 2½") J rectangles and
    1 (1⅞") K square.
- Cut 1 (3¼" x 21") strip.
  Subcut into 6 (3¼") B squares.
- Cut 1 (2⅞" x 21") strip.
  Subcut into 5 (2⅞") D squares.

From coordinating binding fabric:
- Cut 5 (2¼" by fabric width) strips.

From gray solid:
- Cut 6 (1⅞" by fabric width) strips.
  Subcut into 114 (1⅞") E squares and
    12 (1½") O squares.
- Cut 17 (2½" by fabric width) strips.
  Subcut into 37 (2½" x 4½") F rectangles,
    37 (2½" x 8½") G rectangles and
    52 (2½") I squares.
- Cut 2 (5¼" by fabric width) strips.
  Subcut into 10 (5¼") H squares and
    3 (2⅞") L squares.
- Cut 5 (1½" by fabric width) M/N strips.

Completing the Flying Geese Units

1. Draw a diagonal line from corner to corner on the wrong side of each D and E square.

2. Select one B square and four E squares to complete four B-E Flying Geese units for one block.

3. Place an E square right sides together on opposite corners of B and stitch ¼" on both sides of the drawn lines as shown in Figure 1.

Figure 1   Figure 2

4. Cut apart on the marked lines and press seams toward E as shown in Figure 2.

5. With right sides together, lay another marked E square right sides together on the B corner of one stitched unit and stitch ¼" on each side of the marked line referring to Figure 3.

Figure 3   Figure 4

6. Cut the stitched unit on the marked line to make two B-E Flying Geese units as shown in Figure 4; press seams toward E.

7. Repeat steps 5 and 6 with the remaining pieced unit and the remaining E square to complete two more B-E units for a total of four units for one block.

8. Repeat to make a total of 27 sets of four matching B-E units (108 units total), as shown in Figure 5. Set aside remaining E squares for half-star units.

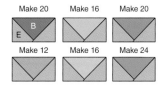

Make 20   Make 16   Make 20
Make 12   Make 16   Make 24

Figure 5

9. Repeat steps 2–7 with D and H squares to make a total of 10 sets of four matching D-H units (28 units total) referring to Figure 6.

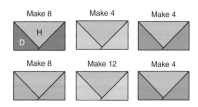

Make 8   Make 4   Make 4
Make 8   Make 12   Make 4

Figure 6

10. To make the J-O Flying Geese units for the side half-star units, draw a diagonal line from corner to corner on the wrong side of each O square.

11. Place an O square right sides together on one corner of J and stitch on the marked line; trim seam to ¼" and press O to the right side referring to Figure 7.

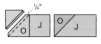

Figure 7   Figure 8

12. Repeat step 11 with a second O square on the remaining end of J to complete one J-O unit referring to Figure 8.

13. Repeat steps 11 and 12 with the remaining J rectangles and O squares to make a total of six J-O units in the color combinations shown in Figure 9.

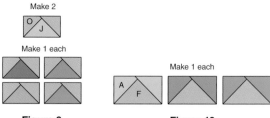

Make 2
Make 1 each
Make 1 each

Figure 9   Figure 10

14. Repeat steps 10–12 with F rectangles and A squares (marked on the diagonal) to make three A-F units in the color combinations shown in Figure 10.

Completing the Star Units

1. Select matching fabric pieces for one star unit as follows: one A square, four C squares and four B-E units.

2. Sew a B-E unit to opposite sides of A to make the center row as shown in Figure 11; press.

Make 2

Figure 11   Figure 12

3. Sew a C square to the short ends of each remaining B-E unit to make the top and bottom rows referring to Figure 12: press.

4. Sew the top and bottom rows to the center row to complete one star unit as shown in Figure 13; press.

Figure 13

5. Repeat steps 1–4 to complete a total of 27 star units referring to Figure 14 for the number to make of each color.

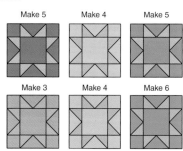

Make 5   Make 4   Make 5
Make 3   Make 4   Make 6

Figure 14

Completing the Framed Star Blocks

1. Select one star unit and two each F and G rectangles.

2. Sew F to opposite sides and G to the top and bottom of the star unit to complete one Framed Star block referring to Figure 15; press.

Figure 15

3. Repeat steps 1 and 2 to complete a total of 17 Framed Star blocks referring to Figure 16 for the number to make in each color.

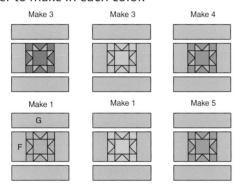

Figure 16

Completing the Star-in-a-Star Blocks

1. Select a set of four matching D-H units, a star unit to match the D-H units, and four I squares to make one Star-in-a-Star block.

2. Sew a D-H unit to opposite sides of the star unit to make the center row as shown in Figure 17; press.

Figure 17

Figure 18

3. Sew an I square to each end of each remaining D-H unit to make the top and bottom rows referring to Figure 18; press.

4. Sew the top and bottom rows to opposite long sides of the center row to complete one Star-in-Star block as shown in Figure 19; press.

Figure 19

5. Repeat steps 1–4 to complete a total of 10 Star-in-a-Star blocks referring to Figure 20 for the number to make in each color.

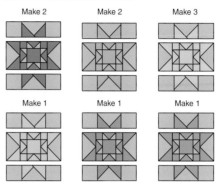

Figure 20

Completing the Half-Star Units

1. Draw a diagonal line from corner to corner on the wrong side of each L square.

2. Referring to Figure 21, place a marked E square right sides together with a K square and stitch ¼" on each side of the marked line. Cut apart on the marked line and press open to make two E-K units.

Figure 21

3. Repeat step 2 to make a total of 12 E-K units referring to Figure 22 for the number to make in each color.

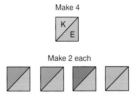

Figure 22

4. Repeat step 2 with D and L squares to make a total of six D-L units referring to Figure 23 for the number to make in each color.

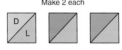

Figure 23

5. Select matching units and pieces as follows to make one half-star unit; one each J rectangle and J-O unit, two E-K units and two C squares.

6. Sew E-K units to opposite short ends of J; press. Sew C to opposite ends of the J-O unit; press. Join the two pieced units to make a half-star unit as shown in Figure 24; press.

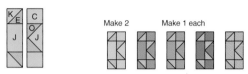

Figure 24   **Figure 25**

7. Repeat to make a total of six half-star units referring to Figure 25.

8. Select matching units and pieces as follows to make a half Star-in-a-Star unit: one half-star unit, two D-L units, one A-F unit and two I squares.

9. Referring to Figure 26, sew a D-L unit to opposite ends of the half-star unit; press. Sew an I square to opposite ends of the A-F unit; press. Join the two pieced units to complete one half Star-in-a-Star unit; press.

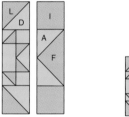

Figure 26   **Figure 27**

10. Repeat steps 8 and 9 to complete a total of three half Star-in-a-Star units referring to Figure 27.

11. Select one half-star unit, one G rectangle and two I squares to complete one half Framed Star unit.

12. Sew an I square to opposite ends of the half-star unit and add G to complete one half Framed Star unit referring to Figure 28; press.

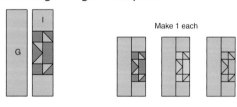

Figure 28   **Figure 29**

13. Repeat steps 11 and 12 to complete a total of three half Framed Star units referring to Figure 29.

Completing the Quilt

1. Arrange and join the Star-in-a-Star and Framed Star blocks with the half Star-in-a-Star and half Framed Star units in rows to complete the pieced center referring to the Assembly Diagram for positioning of blocks and units; press.

2. Join the M/N strips on the short ends to make a long strip; press. Subcut strip into two 1½" x 42½" M strips and two 1½" x 48½" N strips.

3. Sew the M strips to opposite sides and N strips to the top and bottom of the pieced center to complete the quilt top; press.

4. Create a quilt sandwich referring to Finishing Your Quilt on page 48.

5. Quilt as desired.

6. Bind referring to Finishing Your Quilt on page 48 to finish. ■

COLOR KEY
- Blue polka dot
- Blue solid
- Green vine print
- Light green
- Aqua/orange print
- Blue floral
- Gray solid

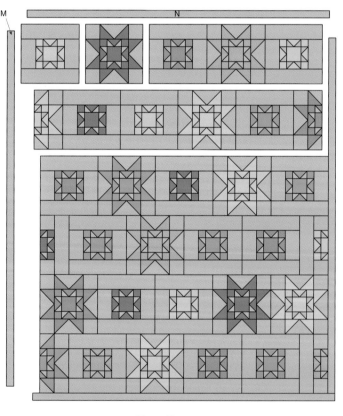

Starry Dance
Assembly Diagram 42" x 50"

Six, Slashed Quilt

Designed & Quilted by Missy Shepler

Six fat quarters, a background fabric and this slash-and-stitch technique will give you a gorgeous original quilt.

Specifications

Skill Level: Confident Beginner
Quilt Size: 56" x 70"

Materials

- 6 fat quarters coordinating cotton fabrics
- ⅝ yard coordinating binding fabric
- 2¾ yards white solid
- Backing to size
- Batting to size
- Thread
- Basic sewing tools and supplies

Cutting

From each fat quarter:

- Cut 4 (1" x 21") strips.

From coordinating binding fabric:

- Cut 7 (2¼" by fabric width) binding strips.

From white solid:

- Cut 1 (70½" by fabric width) strip.
  Subcut into 1 each 6½" x 70½" B strip and 16½" x 70½" A strip and 5 (2½" x 70½") C strips.
- Cut several 4½" by fabric width D strips.
  Subcut into 10 strips of various lengths from 4" to 12".

Completing the Strip Sections

1. Gather the uncut remainders of fat quarters and the 1" x 21" strips.

2. Place four different 1" x 21" strips on each uncut background fat quarter, making sure strips are not the same color as the background fat quarter.

3. Referring to Figure 1 and working with one background fat quarter and a set of four strips at a time, loosely plan arrangement by placing the strips on top of the background at different angles without being parallel to the long edge of the background fat quarter.

Figure 1

4. Move the strips aside, and using a rotary cutter and ruler on your cutting mat, slice the background fabric into two pieces where you want the first strip to appear, as shown in Figure 2.

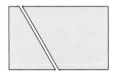

Figure 2

5. With right sides together and matching raw edges, align and stitch the long edge of the first strip with the cut edge of one of the pieces cut in step 4 referring to Figure 3; press to set the seam and then press the seam open or away from the strip.

Figure 3

6. Repeat step 5, sewing the remaining long edge of the first strip to the cut edge of the second piece cut in step 4 to complete the insertion of one strip as shown in Figure 4.

Figure 4

7. To complete the strip section, repeat steps 4–6 to insert each of the remaining strips one at a time, placing strips at different angles, crossing strips for extra variety referring to Figure 5.

Figure 5

8. Repeat steps 4–7 with remaining background fat quarters and strips to complete six strip sections.

9. Trim the long sides of each strip section straight as shown in Figure 6. Trim as needed to make 13½"-tall square-cornered rectangles.

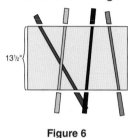

Figure 6

Here's a Tip

To avoid losing too much fabric width, realign the second-cut fabric section when joining it to the strip. With right sides together, pinch or pin one edge along the seam allowance; then flip the fabric open to see if the edges align. Adjust as needed before sewing the seam.

10. Cut each strip section into three 4½" by the length of the strip sections referring to Figure 7. ***Note:*** *See Tip for more cutting options.*

Figure 7

Completing the Quilt

1. Select and join three different-fabric strip sections on the short ends to make a long strip; press. Repeat to make a total of six pieced strips.

2. Select and sew D strips to each end of each strip. Trim each strip to 4½" x 70½" leaving different lengths of D at ends of strips.

3. Join the pieced strips with the A, B and C strips to complete the quilt top referring to the Assembly Diagram for positioning; press.

4. Create a quilt sandwich referring to Finishing Your Quilt on page 48.

5. Quilt as desired.

6. Bind referring to Finishing Your Quilt on page 48 to finish. ■

"Some days I just want to sew. No pattern, no plan—just a few fun hours with fabric and thread. This quilt goes together quickly and is perfect for 'just sew' sessions. The improv strip piecing provides plenty of opportunity for experimentation. There is something relaxing about it—no worries about points and perfect patches. Just slash and sew!" —Missy Shepler

Here's a Tip

Measure the width of the narrowest strip section. If the narrowest strip section measures 13½" or greater, use a strip width of 4½". If the narrowest strip measures less than 13½", divide that width by three and round the measurement down to the nearest ⅛" or ¼". This will be the width to cut all strips.

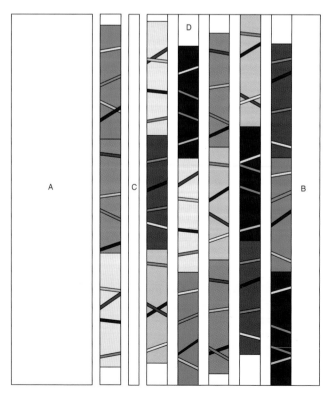

Six, Slashed Quilt
Assembly Diagram 56" x 70"

Persian Rug

Designed & Quilted by Wendy Sheppard

Put your fat quarters to work creating this cute table runner.
Your fabric choices will change its appearance, so explore!

Specifications

Skill Level: Intermediate
Runner Size: 32" x 15"
Block Size: 6" x 6" finished
Number of Blocks: 3

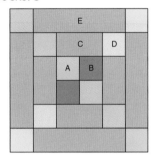

Framed Four-Patch
6" x 6" Finished Block
Make 3

Materials

- 1 fat quarter each yellow floral, yellow tile print, cream/blue vine print, gray solid, gray floral, blue large floral
- ⅓ yard coordinating binding fabric
- Backing to size
- Batting to size
- Thread
- Basic sewing tools and supplies

Cutting

From yellow floral:

- Cut 2 (1½" x 21") strips.
    Subcut into 18 (1½") A squares.
- Cut 5 (1¾" x 21") strips.
    Subcut 2 strips into 2 (1¾" x 11½") O strips.
    Set aside remaining strips for N.

From yellow tile print:

- Cut 1 (1½" x 21") strip.
    Subcut into 12 (1½") D squares.
- Cut 1 (4⅛" x 21") strip.
    Subcut into 1 (4⅛") square. Cut the square on both diagonals to make 4 K triangles.
    Trim the remainder of the strip to 2½" and subcut into 4 (2½") H squares.

From cream/blue vine print:

- Cut 1 (4⅛" x 21") strip.
    Subcut into 3 (4⅛") squares. Cut each square on both diagonals to make 12 G triangles.

From gray solid:

- Cut 5 (1½" x 21") strips.
    Subcut into 12 (1½" x 2½") C rectangles and 12 (1½" x 4½") E rectangles.
- Cut 9 (¾" x 21") strips.
    Subcut into 2 strips each ¾" x 9" L and ¾" x 12" P. Set aside remaining 7 strips for M/Q.

From gray floral:

- Cut 1 (1½" x 21") strip.
    Subcut into 6 (1½") B squares.
- Cut 2 (2½" x 21") strips.
    Subcut into 4 (2½") I squares and 4 (2½" x 4⅞") rectangles. Trim 1 end of each rectangle at a 45-degree angle as shown in Figure 1 to make J pieces.
- Cut 1 (2½" x 21") strip.
    Subcut into 4 (2½" x 5") F rectangles.

45-degree angle

Figure 1

From blue large floral:

- Cut 6 (2" x 21") strips.
    Subcut 2 strips into 2 (2" x 12½") R strips. Set aside remaining strips for S.

From coordinating binding fabric:

- Cut 3 (2¼" by fabric width) binding strips.

Completing the Blocks

1. Select two B, four D and six A squares, and four each C and E rectangles to make one Framed Four-Patch block.

2. Join two each A and B squares as shown in Figure 2 to make an A-B unit; press.

3. Sew a C rectangle to opposite sides of the A-B unit to make center unit as shown in Figure 3; press.

Figure 2

Figure 3

4. Sew A to one end and D to the opposite end of one C rectangle to make an A-C-D unit; press. Repeat to make a second unit. Stitch the A-C-D units to the long edges of the center unit, again referring to Figure 3; press.

5. Sew E to opposite sides of the previously stitched unit referring to Figure 4; press.

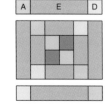

Figure 4

6. Sew an A square to one end and a D square to the opposite end of two E rectangles to make two A-D-E units; press. Sew these units to the long sides of the previously pieced unit to complete one Framed Four-Patch block, again referring to Figure 4; press.

7. Repeat steps 1–6 to complete a total of three Framed Four-Patch blocks.

Completing the Runner

1. Sew H to I to G and then add J and G to make a side unit as shown in Figure 5; press. Repeat to make a total of four side units.

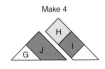

Figure 5   Figure 6

2. Sew K to one side and G to the opposite side of an F rectangle, aligning K and G with one square end of F, referring to Figure 6; press.

3. Trim F even with the edges of G and K to make a 90-degree corner and complete one corner unit as shown in Figure 7.

Make 2

Figure 7

4. Repeat steps 2 and 3 to complete a second corner unit.

5. Repeat steps 2 and 3 to make two reverse corner units referring to Figure 8.

Reverse Make 2

Figure 8

Here's a Tip

Apply spray starch to the F and J rectangles before trimming ends to help stabilize bias edges. Handle edges carefully after trimming to avoid stretching.

6. Arrange and join the Framed Four-Patch blocks with the side, corner and reverse corner units referring to the Assembly Diagram; press.

7. Sew L strips to opposite short ends of the pieced center; press seams toward L.

8. Join the M/Q strips on the short ends to make a long strip; press. Subcut strip into two ¾" x 26½" M strips and two ¾" x 29½" Q strips.

9. Sew M strips to opposite long sides of the pieced center; press seams toward M strips.

10. Join the N strips on the short ends to make a long strip; press. Subcut strip into two 1¾" x 29" N strips. Sew N strips to opposite long sides of the pieced center; press seams toward N strips.

11. Sew O strips to opposite short ends of the pieced center; press.

12. Sew P strips to short ends and Q strips to opposite long sides of the pieced center; press seams toward P and Q strips.

13. Sew R strips to the short ends of the pieced center; press seams toward R strips.

14. Join S strips on short ends to make a long strip; press. Subcut strip into two 1" x 32½" S strips. Sew S strips to opposite long sides of the pieced center to complete the runner top; press seams toward S strips.

15. Create a quilt sandwich referring to Finishing Your Quilt on page 48.

16. Quilt as desired.

17. Bind referring to Finishing Your Quilt on page 48 to finish. ■

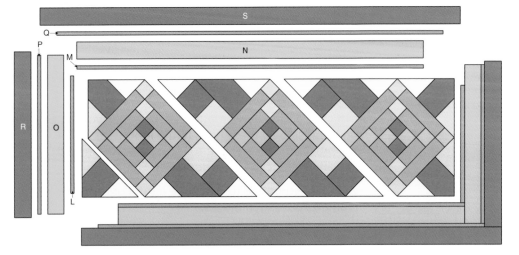

Persian Rug
Assembly Diagram 32" x 15"

"The fabric choices that made up the blocks reminded me of the Persian geometric tiles, thus the name Persian Rug." —Wendy Sheppard

Mountain High Table Set

Designed & Quilted by Gina Gempesaw

This easy bargello look can be accomplished using six fat quarters to make two place mats and the runner.

Specifications
Skill Level: Confident Beginner
Runner Size: 60½" x 13¼"
Place Mat Size: 17" x 13¼"

Materials
- 1 fat quarter each dark blue tonal, blue floral, green print, light blue tonal, light green print, white floral
- ½ yard medium blue tonal
- ⅔ yard dark blue tonal
- Backing to size
- Batting to size
- Thread
- Basic sewing tools and supplies

Project Note
The segments are arranged in a different pattern in the place mats and runner. The pattern is formed by joining the segments in tubes, opening different seams in each tube and removing one segment from the end of the resulting strip. Decide on the pattern before you begin and lay out the segments as they are created to make sure you maintain the design.

Cutting

From each fat quarter:
- Cut 6 (2¾" x 21") A strips.

From medium blue tonal:
- Cut 3 (1½" by fabric width) B/C strips.
- Cut 4 (1½" by fabric width) D/E strips.

From dark blue tonal:
- Cut 8 (2¼" by fabric width) binding strips.

Completing the Bargello Strips
1. Assign numbers 1–6 to the fat quarters. Select and join one A strip from each fat quarter to make a strip set; press strip seams as indicated by arrows in Figure 1. Repeat to make a total of six strip sets.

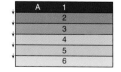

Figure 1

2. With right sides together, join the bottom and top A strips of one strip set to make a tube as shown in Figure 2; finger-press seam toward strip 6.

Figure 2

3. Subcut the stitched tube into 10 (2") A segments as shown in Figure 3.

Figure 3

4. Repeat steps 2 and 3 with all strip sets.

Completing the Place Mats
1. Select 10 segments for one place mat. Undo the stitches in seam between fabrics 1 and 6, and open the strip; remove strip 6 to make the first strip (on

the left-hand side) as shown in Figure 4. Repeat to make a total of three identical strips.

Figure 4   Figure 5

2. Repeat step 1, opening the seam between fabrics 5 and 6, and remove strip 5 to make the second strip as shown in Figure 5. Repeat to make a total of three identical strips.

3. Repeat this process, opening seams between strips and removing segments to complete the segments needed to complete the pattern referring to Figure 6.

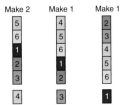

Figure 6

4. Arrange and join the segments referring to the Assembly Diagram to complete the place mat center; press seams to one side.

5. Join the B/C strips on the short ends to make a long strip; subcut strip into four 1½" x 15½" B strips and four 1½" x 13¾" C strips.

6. Sew a B strip to opposite long sides and C strips to the short ends of the place mat center to complete the place mat top; press seams toward strips.

7. Create a quilt sandwich referring to Finishing Your Quilt on page 48.

8. Quilt as desired.

9. Bind referring to Finishing Your Quilt on page 48 to finish.

10. Repeat steps 1–4 and 6–9 to complete a second place mat. Set aside remainder of binding for runner.

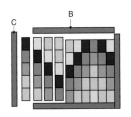

Mountain High Place Mat
Assembly Diagram 17" x 13¼"

Completing the Runner

1. Referring to instructions for Completing the Place Mats, select 32 A segments and undo stitches, removing segments as shown in Figure 7.

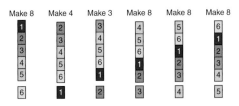

Figure 7

2. Arrange and join the segments referring to the Assembly Diagram to complete the runner center; press.

3. Join the D/E strips on short ends to make a long strip; subcut strip into two 1½" x 59" D strips and two 1½" x 13¾" E strips.

4. Sew D strips to opposite long sides and E strips to opposite short ends to complete the runner top; press seams toward strips.

5. Create a quilt sandwich referring to Finishing Your Quilt on page 48.

6. Quilt as desired.

7. Bind referring to Finishing Your Quilt on page 48 to finish. ■

"I love bargello quilts. It was a challenge to make a version of a bargello using just the six fat quarters." —Gina Gempesaw

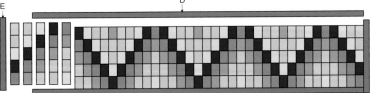

Mountain High Runner
Assembly Diagram 60½" x 13¼"

Here's a Tip

A design wall or flat surface is a lifesaver when stitching bargello projects. Stitching the units together two at a time and pinning them in position on the design wall prevents units from being stitched in the wrong order.

Finishing Your Quilt

1. Press quilt top on both sides; check for proper seam pressing and trim all loose threads.

2. Sandwich batting between the stitched top and the prepared backing piece; pin or baste layers together to hold. Mark quilting design and quilt as desired by hand or machine.

3. When quilting is complete, remove pins or basting. Trim batting and backing fabric edges even with raw edges of quilt top.

4. Join binding strips on short ends with diagonal seams to make one long strip; trim seams to ¼" and press seams open.

5. Fold the binding strip in half with wrong sides together along length; press.

6. Sew binding to quilt edges, matching raw edges, mitering corners and overlapping ends.

7. Fold binding to the back side and stitch in place to finish.

Special Thanks

Please join us in thanking the talented designers whose work is featured in this collection.

Gina Gempesaw
Mountain High Table Set, page 45
Train Tracks, page 9

Bev Getschel
Raining Boxes, page 20

Connie Kauffman
A Lapful of Empty Spools, page 24

Tricia Lynn Maloney
Sassy Classy Tote, page 12
Wingnuts, page 3

Jenny Rekeweg
The Shuffle, page 6

Nancy Scott
Stunning Stars, page 17

Missy Shepler
Six, Slashed Quilt, page 39

Wendy Sheppard
Persian Rug, page 42
Starry Dance, page 34

Jackie White
Bountiful Bloom, page 28

Annie's® *Fat Quarter Shuffle* is published by Annie's, 306 East Parr Road, Berne, IN 46711. Printed in USA. Copyright © 2013, 2014 Annie's. All rights reserved. This publication may not be reproduced in part or in whole without written permission from the publisher.

RETAIL STORES: If you would like to carry this pattern book or any other Annie's publication, visit AnniesWSL.com.

Every effort has been made to ensure that the instructions in this pattern book are complete and accurate. We cannot, however, take responsibility for human error, typographical mistakes or variations in individual work. Please visit AnniesCustomerCare.com to check for pattern updates.

ISBN: 978-1-59635-666-5
2 3 4 5 6 7 8 9